A Christmas Carol

Gary Owen won the George Devine and Meyer-Whitworth Awards for his play *The Shadow of a Boy* (National Theatre), and the Pearson Best Play Award and a Fringe First for *The Drowned World* (Paines Plough). Other plays include *Crazy Gary's Mobile Disco* (Paines Plough and Sgript Cymru), *Cancer Time* (Theatre 503), *Ghost City* (Sgript Cymru), *Amgen: Broken* (Sherman Cymru), *We That Are Left* and *Mrs Reynolds and The Ruffian* (both Watford Palace Theatre). Gary is currently working on new plays for the National Theatre of Scotland and National Theatre Wales, and is co-creator and writer of an original series for BBC Wales called *The Fabulous Baker Boys*.

Charles Dickens

A Christmas Carol

adaptation by Gary Owen

Methuen Drama

Published by Methuen Drama 2009

1 3 5 7 9 10 8 6 4 2

Methuen Drama
A & C Black Publishers Ltd
36 Soho Square
London W1D 3QY
www.methuendrama.com

ISBN 978 1 408 12946 3

A CIP catalogue record for this book is available
from the British Library

Typeset by Country Setting, Kingsdown, Kent
Printed and bound in Great Britain by
CPI Cox and Wyman, Reading, Berkshire

This book is produced using paper that is made from wood grown
in managed, sustainable forests. It is natural, renewable and recyclable.
The logging and manufacturing processes conform to the environmental
regulations of the country of origin.

A Christmas Carol

This adaptation of *A Christmas Carol* premiered at Sherman, Cardiff, on 4 December 2009. The cast was as follows:

Fezziwig/Ghost of Christmas Future/ Peter Cratchit/Smart Gentleman	Matthew Bulgo
Scrooge	Mark Frost
Bob Cratchit/Constable	Simon Ludders
Matron/Housekeeper/Fine Lady/ Mrs Fezziwig/Want	Sharon Morgan
Marley/Ghost of Christmas Present/ Ignorance	Simon Nehan
Tiny Tim/Fred/Dick/Young Scrooge/ Sammy/Boy/Musician (*accordion*)	David Osmond
Match Girl/Ghost of Christmas Past/ Martha Cratchit/Fred's Wife/Musician	Elin Phillips
Belle/Young Scrooge's Mother/ Mrs Cratchit	Amy Ellen Richardson

Director Amy Hodge
Designer Patrick Burnier
Lighting Designer Emma Chapman
Composer (*Songs*) *and Sound Designer* Adrienne Quartly
Musical Director, Orchestrations and Composer (*Music*) Michael Cryne
Choreographer and Movement Director Aline David
Puppet Maker and Trainer Michael Fowkes
Assistant Director Sarah Bickerton

Characters

Match Girl
Jacob Marley
Bob Cratchit
Smart Gentleman
Ebenezer Scrooge
Sammy
Fine Lady
Fred
Ghost of Christmas Past
Constable
Scrooge's Mother
Young Scrooge
Matron
Dick Wilkins
Fezziwig
Mrs Fezziwig
Belle
Boy/Ignorance
Girl/Want
Ghost of Christmas Present
Mrs Cratchit
Martha Cratchit
Peter Cratchit
Tiny Tim
Ghost of Christmas Future
Housekeeper
Fred's Wife
Boy

Act One

Christmas Eve, 1843. London. People striding, bustling, going about their business, all very impatient and fraught – customers haggling with traders, boys running errands, a **Match Girl***, trying to sell matches to everyone but having no luck –*

– and moving among them, **Jacob Marley***.*

Marley *looks subtly different to everyone else. And he moves differently: he darts across the stage, looking here, peering there, passing within inches of people, but no one notices him, no one says a thing.*

Marley *is watching. He's watching people going about their ordinary, everyday business, trying to discern something – but what? He's at the front of stage, his back to the audience, apparently absorbed in the scene before him –*

– and then he spins round and stares right at us.

Marley   Well, look at you. Ladies and gentlemen, boys and girls, lords and larcenists. I have a question. How many of you have ever seen a ghost?

Beat.

All of you. Every single last one. You're looking at a ghost right now. Because I, Jacob Marley, am a dead man. And let me tell you, being dead is no fun. Your body falls apart, there are maggots and worms crawling round inside you, it's so itchy –

He's trying to scratch an itch on his shoulder, but he can't quite reach . . .

– if you'll excuse me.

And he pulls his right hand clean out of its socket!

That should do the trick!

Then, using his detached right hand as an improvised back-scratcher, he has a good scratch.

What a relief!

His itching dealt with, **Marley** *returns the hand to its socket.*

I've been dead seven long years. They put me in the ground, bid me rest in peace – but there was no rest for me. I just couldn't sleep. So I got up, climbed out of my grave. I've been wandering the earth all this time trying to figure out, what did I do wrong?

Bob Cratchit *enters, just in time to see the* **Match Girl** *being brushed off by someone else who doesn't want to buy her matches.* **Bob** *is obviously troubled by the* **Match Girl**'s *broken demeanour. The* **Match Girl** *goes up to a* **Smart Gentleman**.

Match Girl   Will you buy of box of matches, sir? Only a penny.

Smart Gentleman   I have all the matches I need.

Match Girl   But my family need the money!

She clings to the **Smart Gentleman**'s *arm.*

Smart Gentleman   Get off me, you wretch!

He pushes her off – she stumbles and falls.

Bob Cratchit *rushes to the* **Match Girl**.

Marley   I did what I was supposed to – I lived a decent life – I died a rich man.

Bob Cratchit   Let me help you.

Match Girl   Thank you, sir.

Bob Cratchit   Merry Christmas, young lady! And every good wish of the season to you.

The **Match Girl** *cannot help but smile.*

Match Girl   Merry Christmas to you, sir.

Marley *watches this exchange – how the* **Match Girl** *is transformed by* **Bob Cratchit**'s *simple kindness.*

Marley   And there it is! That's what I got wrong! In the hurry to make all my money, I forgot to be kind!

Calls of 'Merry Christmas!' and friendly greetings ripple out from **Bob Cratchit** *and the* **Match Girl** *to the whole crowd.*

Marley   And look, it only takes one person to be kind – and everything changes. The gift is given onward, one to the other –

The whole mood has changed, the movement is less frenetic, more elegant – and a couple of carollers wander on, singing.

Marley   – especially at this time of year. Christmas gives us every excuse to be kind – if kindness is in our nature.

Marley*'s attention moves from* **Bob Cratchit** *and the* **Match Girl**, *back to us.*

Marley   Today, by the way, is Christmas Eve, 1843. Victoria is on the throne – the one who was frequently not amused – and this is London – just in case you are confused. And though the wind is cold and the night is dark, the spirit of Christmas is at work – charming, cheering, melting hearts.

Bellowed, from offstage:

Scrooge   What d'you mean, 'Merry Christmas'? What nonsense?

Marley   Well . . . perhaps not every heart.

Scrooge *enters and instantly the mood changes. People nearby cower and flee to the far side of the stage.*

Scrooge   Christmas? What flim-flam. What fol-de-rol. What . . .

He's stuck for a word . . . and then it comes to him.

What HUMBUG!

Marley   This is Ebenezer Scrooge. In life, we were business partners. Moneylenders. You needed money, we would lend it to you – at a price.

Scrooge   Christmas! An excuse to spend money you haven't got, you dimwits. Well, spend away, and I'll lend away. And soon – I'll own you all!

Song: 'I'm The Man You Turn To'.

> I'm the man you turn to
> When you need a helping hand.
> I can get you out of trouble
> I can help with life's demands.
> When the pennies are a-pinching
> I can spare a pound or two.
> So if your purse is empty
> Let me see what I can do.
>
> I'm the man you turn to
> When the kids all need new shoes,
> When the rent man comes a-knocking,
> Or you bet your life and lose.
> When your wallet hasn't got it
> And there's no meat for the stew,
> Come and talk to me, my friend,
> I'll see what I can do.
>
> And all I ask in return
> Is that you pay a small sum, weekly,
> And so long as you pay what's due
> I'll thank you, and smile very meekly.

Spoken:

> But, what do you say?
> You can't pay?
> No problem, that's fine,
> These things happen
> All the time . . .

Sung:

> I'll take your bread, I'll take your wine
> I'll take your cows, I'll take your swine
> I'll take your spade, I'll take your pick
> I'll take your mortar and your brick
> I'll take your dog, I'll take your bone
> I'll take your house, I'll take your home
> I'll take everything you own!
> I'll take everything you own!

So . . .

I'm the man you turn to
When you need a helping hand.
I can get you out of trouble,
I can help with life's demands.
When the pennies are a-pinching
I can spare a pound or two.
So if your purse is empty
Let me see what I can do.

Marley   It was me that made Scrooge a moneylender. Before we met, he kept books for a grocer. I taught Scrooge how to make money, from money.

The **Match Girl** *approaches* **Scrooge**.

Match Girl   Book of matches, sir? Just a penny.

Scrooge   A whole penny, for lucifers? Do you mean to rob me, girl?

Match Girl   Please, sir, the rent man's coming, and I'm penniless.

Scrooge (*sensing opportunity*)   Is that so?

Match Girl   My husband's lame from the Afghan war and my littlest is just a babe. I must make a shilling today or the landlord will throw us out.

Scrooge   One pays one's rent or one is evicted; that is the law.

Match Girl   We'll die of the cold! You wouldn't let us freeze, sir – not on Christmas Eve.

Scrooge   Why, no! Not if there were a more profitable resolution we might come to.

Match Girl   Oh, thank you, sir – I think.

She offers a book of matches.

Match Girl   That'll be a penny then. Or maybe you'd like . . . two?

Scrooge   I'm not going to buy your matches, witless child. I'm going to lend you the money.

Match Girl   Lend me the money? I don't know about that . . .

Scrooge   Please yourself. But as you say, it is getting rather chilly. Do babies like the cold?

Match Girl   No, sir, not one bit!

Scrooge   So if you would read the terms of the contract and sign.

Scrooge *whips out a contract (a scroll falling to the floor) and a pen.*

Match Girl   But I can't read, sir. Nor write.

Scrooge   Make a squiggle, or a cross, whatever you like.

Match Girl   If you say so . . .

*The **Match Girl** takes the pen.*

Match Girl   I've done a circle, sir. Like the sun, which I love for / its warmth.

Scrooge (*interrupting*)   Yes, that's all very nice, now here's your shilling.

He hands over a silver coin.

Match Girl   Thank you, sir.

*She calls to **Sammy** (someone else onstage).*

Match Girl   Sammy!

She passes on the silver coin.

Take this home, and see the rent man gets it.

Sammy *runs off.*

Match Girl   I'm ever so grateful, you can't know what this means to a young family . . .

Scrooge   And now my penny.

Match Girl   Sorry, sir?

Scrooge   The penny you owe me? The first instalment of your debt? Payable immediately – as the contract clearly says.

Scrooge *whips out the contract again.*

Marley   Oh dear. The old instant repayment trick. I taught him that.

Scrooge   It's all in the small print.

Match Girl   But I can't read.

Scrooge   Is that my fault?

Match Girl   The whole shilling went on rent – you saw that, sir!

Scrooge   It's no business of mine how you dispose of your funds, young lady –

Match Girl   Very civil of you to say, sir.

Scrooge *(suddenly thundering)*   – but give me the penny you owe me, or I'll have you thrown in prison this instant!

Bob Cratchit   Mr Scrooge, sir, begging your pardon – it is Christmas.

Scrooge *(shouting)*   Constable! Constable of the watch!

Match Girl   Please, there's only me to look after the children.

Scrooge   A whole farthing I paid in tax this year, but still never a peeler about when you need some wretch dragging off to the Marshalsea.

Match Girl   Please, sir. Please don't put me in jail.

Scrooge   Very well – in lieu of payment, give me your boots. Then we're settled, for today.

Match Girl   If I go barefoot, I'll get frostbite. I'll be crippled!

Scrooge   You go barefoot, or you go to prison. You choose, you're a free citizen.

Match Girl   All right, sir.

She slips off her boots, and hands them over. The cold makes her hop from foot to foot.

Scrooge   What a charming little jig. Perhaps you could make a living as a dancing girl, did you ever consider that?

Bob Cratchit   Enough of this! (*To the* **Match Girl**.) Young lady, I'll take a book of matches.

Match Girl   You will? Thank you, sir.

Bob Cratchit   And here's a penny.

Marley   This fine fellow is Bob Cratchit. He works for Scrooge.

Match Girl   Here's your penny, Mr Scrooge. Can I have my boots back?

Scrooge*, none too graciously, thrusts the boots back into her hands. The* **Match Girl** *flees as fast as she can.*

Scrooge   I must be paying you too much, Cratchit, if you've got pennies to be handing out to urchins.

Bob Cratchit   I couldn't see her go barefoot, sir.

Scrooge   What d'you care if some feeble-minded match girl freezes? There's plenty more of them.

Bob Cratchit   Let us say, the spirit of Christmas moved me.

Scrooge   The what of what did what? It's as if you're blabbering on in some jibber-jabber language, as might be spoken by foreigners. Or the Welsh.

Bob Cratchit *gives up trying to explain the real reason for his actions.*

Scrooge   Now – to work! Or I'll dock your pay for time wasted!

Scrooge *and* **Bob Cratchit** *get to work.* **Bob Cratchit** *sits at a desk, trying to warm his hands by a candle,* **Scrooge** *at a huge counting desk, which is itself on a raised platform – getting up into his* *seat involves a bit of a climb. Once seated,* **Scrooge** *towers imperiously above the stage.*

Scrooge   We've got twenty-three eviction notices and sixty final demands to issue before close of business.

Bob Cratchit   Today, sir? Eviction notices on Christmas Eve?

A **Fine Lady** *approaches.*

Fine Lady   Mr Scrooge? Mr Ebenezer Scrooge?

Bob Cratchit   Mr Scrooge? A lady for you.

Scrooge   Can't a man get any peace?

Fine Lady   I am obliged to speak to you on a delicate matter. That matter being, for want of a better word, money.

Scrooge   Money!

The change in the man is instant.

My dear lady, why didn't you say so?

He hops down from his seat.

How are you? How can I be of help? And – how much do you want?

Fine Lady   How much can you spare?

Scrooge   How much can I spare? I'm the richest man in the world, I can spare more than your little lady's mind can possibly imagine.

Fine Lady   Clearly I can't take all your money, Mr Scrooge. But shall I put you down for a donation / of say . . .

Scrooge (*interrupting*)   What? What did you say?

Fine Lady   I said, 'donation' . . .

Scrooge *sways as if faint.*

Scrooge   Cratchit! Assist me!

Bob Cratchit *runs and places a seat beneath* **Scrooge**. *He collapses into it.*

Scrooge   Madam, I am not accustomed to hearing such language!

Fine Lady   We are fighting Ignorance and Want, establishing homes for children who have no families, and who otherwise would grow up on the streets.

Scrooge   Forgive me: are there not prisons?

Fine Lady   There are, Mr Scrooge, filled with souls whose only crime is poverty.

Scrooge   Are there not also workhouses?

Fine Lady   Yes, dreadful places where families are torn apart!

Scrooge   Then surely, madam, the poor have all the provision they need.

Fine Lady   Every winter, children die from cold and hunger.

Scrooge   All they better if they do.

Fine Lady   You would let the poor die?

Scrooge   Surplus population is the scourge of the Empire. High time we thinned out the herd.

The **Fine Lady** *is gobsmacked.* **Fred**, **Scrooge**'s *nephew, enters.*

Fred   Merry Christmas, Bob.

Bob Cratchit   Merry Christmas to you, sir.

Fine Lady   Mr Scrooge, I am scandalised. I don't know what to say.

Scrooge   Well then, pray toddle off, and let me get back to making money.

Fred (*to* **Bob**)   Any chance of a word with my uncle?

Bob Cratchit   Mr Scrooge! Your nephew to see you.

Scrooge   Oh, now what . . .

Fred   Merry Christmas, Uncle.

Scrooge   I wouldn't be so merry if I were as poor as you.

Fred   And I wouldn't be so grim if I were even a tenth as rich as you are! Now, why don't you join the family for Christmas Day?

Scrooge   Every year you invite me for Christmas.

Fred   Yes, I do.

Scrooge   And every year, what do I say?

Fred (*doing an impression*)   You say 'Christmas? What silliness! What tomfoolery! What HUMBUG!'

Bob Cratchit *is much amused by this – till* **Scrooge** *shoots him a look.*

Scrooge   Then why haven't you learned not to waste your breath? And how do you afford / all this feasting, young Fred?

Bob Cratchit *tries to interrupt the discussion before it gets any nastier.*

Fred   We'll have games, and songs, and sweetmeats – and oh! You should see the turkey. A magnificent beast. We'll be eating it till Easter.

Scrooge   Your wife came to me looking for a loan last week. Perhaps prudence would be a better gift than sweetmeats.

Fred *clearly didn't know this.*

Bob Cratchit   Mr Scrooge! Mr Scrooge!

Scrooge   I am plagued on all sides!

Bob Cratchit   Mr Scrooge, might I just have one piece of coal for my fire?

Scrooge   No!

Bob Cratchit   My hands are so cold I can barely write. If I can't write, I can't send out eviction notices.

Scrooge   Well, if you can't do your job, then consider yourself sacked.

Bob Cratchit   Mr Scrooge! For pity's sake. It is Christmas!

Scrooge   That's it! I have heard enough of Christmas!

Song: 'Bah! Humbug! It's Christmas!'

Christmas comes but once a year
And once is once too many
They say it is a time of cheer
A day for good and plenty
But I say it's a maddening time
When man abandons reason
And that is why I can't abide
This hideous Christmas season.

You may not like your mother,
You may hate your dear old dad,
At Christmas you invite them round
And pretend that you are glad.
They scoff up all your turkey
They knock back your wine and beer
And all they say in thanks is that
The gravy tasted queer.

Christmas comes but once a year
And once is once too many
They say it is a time of cheer
A day for good and plenty
But I say it's a maddening time
When man abandons reason
And that is why I can't abide
This hideous Christmas season.

You may not have a penny
You may scrimp and dress in rags.
At Christmas the kids pester you,
Load up your shopping bags.
They never want what they have got,
They don't appreciate.
Then January the first you've got
The bailiffs at your gate.

Christmas comes but once a year
And once is once too many
They say it is a time of cheer
A day for good and plenty
But I say it's a maddening time
When man abandons reason
And that is why I can't abide
This hideous Christmas season.

Fine Lady   I'll find some Christmas spirit elsewhere, I'm sure. Good day to you, sir.

She leaves.

Fred   You will always be welcome at our home, Uncle: but if that is truly how you feel, then I shan't trouble you. Ever again.

He too departs.

Scrooge   And good riddance.

Bob Cratchit   Mr Scrooge, sir . . .

Scrooge   I suppose you'll be wanting the day off tomorrow? For Christmas?

Bob Cratchit   If it's convenient, sir.

Scrooge   You can have the day off – but no pay!

Bob Cratchit   I promised my children a proper Christmas dinner!

Scrooge   I don't care if your children eat at Christmas or any other day!

Marley   It strikes me now that if kindness can start with one good man, then perhaps one cruel man can bring kindness to an end.

Scrooge   I recall in old Oliver Cromwell's time, they banned Christmas.

Marley   Perhaps one *very* cruel man could even bring Christmas to an end –

Scrooge   I might buy myself a few Members of Parliament, see if we can try that trick again! What d'you say, Bob?

Marley   – especially if that cruel man is also the richest man in the world!

Bob Cratchit   I say, a very merry Christmas to you, sir.

Scrooge   Say it while you still can.

Bob Cratchit *flees.* **Scrooge** *climbs down from his throne.*

Marley   And it was me that helped make him the richest man in the world! No wonder I can't sleep.

Scrooge *prepares to leave the office.*

Scrooge   Yes . . . 'An Act for the Banning of Christmas'. I like the sound of that. And MPs can be bought for the price of a duck house.

Marley   And so Scrooge wends his way home. Happy – well, not happy – resolved, then, to spend Christmas Day alone. He lives in dank offices, lost in the fog of the river.

Marley   Ebenezer Scrooge!

Scrooge *turns.*

Scrooge   Jacob Marley!

Marley   Yes.

Scrooge   You're still alive! You didn't die after all!

Marley   I am Jacob Marley. I was your partner. And I have been dead these seven years.

Scrooge   Next thing you'll be telling me you're a ghost!

Marley   I *am* a ghost.

Scrooge   Nonsense! I see you, standing before me, lively as I am.

Marley   If I am a real living man, greet me as you would a real living man. Shake my hand.

And **Marley** *extends his right hand.* **Scrooge** *takes it – and* **Marley***'s hand comes out of its socket.* **Scrooge** *doesn't notice and keeps pumping away.*

Scrooge   It's good to see you, my friend, and good to shake your hand again.

Marley   Good to see you too, old chum.

Marley *raises his unhanded arm, and waves at* **Scrooge***.*

Scrooge *looks down and realises he's shaking a detached hand.*

Marley   The living are surrounded by spirits, Scrooge. They hover around you, watching, listening, learning. Spirits of the dead. Spirits of dream. Spirits of other ages.

Scrooge   There are no mysterious beings from other ages, watching us.

Marley (*pointing at the audience*)   They sit before you.

Scrooge   What humbug!

Marley   Can't you see them? Can't you hear them?

Scrooge   I see only you, my friend Jacob Marley. I hear – nothing.

Marley (*to the audience*)   When I give the word, I want you to wail like a ghost, or scream like a spook, or roar like a monster. Now – make some noise!

Scrooge   I am a rational man, and this is a rational age.

Marley (*to the audience*)   Louder!

Scrooge   There are no such things as spirits!

Marley (*to the audience*)   Louder still! (*To* **Scrooge**.) Do you hear them, Scrooge?

Scrooge   Yes, yes, I hear them. So it's true. There are ghosts, and spirits all around. Sir ghost, I beg of you, please don't hurt me, I'm a humble man who tries to lead an honest life . . .

Marley   Scrooge?

Scrooge   What?

Marley   Can I have my hand back?

Scrooge *edges closer to* **Marley** *– then slaps the detached hand down in* **Marley***'s good hand, and retreats as far as he can to the other side of the stage.*

Scrooge   I'm sure you have many ghoulish duties to fulfil, please don't let me keep you.

Marley   Don't you want to know about these chains?

Scrooge   They do look heavy.

Marley   They are my punishment.

Scrooge   Punishment? For what?

Marley   For the way I lived my life.

Scrooge*'s outrage gets the better of his fear.*

Scrooge   But you lived an exemplary life! A wonderful life!

Marley   Far from it.

Scrooge   It was businessmen such as you, Marley, who made London the engine of the Empire. You should be celebrated, not punished!

Marley   You call me a businessman – my only business was profit.

Scrooge   I think the worms have grown fat on your brain, old friend.

Marley   Let in the spirit of Christmas. Let in warmth, and light, and love. Live every day with the spirit of Christmas in your heart – and you may yet be saved.

Scrooge   Ghosts I might believe in, given evidence. But that my friend Jacob Marley should become a Liberal – it's too much to stomach. Spirit – I don't believe you're even real. I thought one of the potatoes at lunch looked a bit off. That's all this vision is – gas from a green potato.

Marley   If you will not listen to me, your old friend – then I will call upon my new friends.

Scrooge   And who are your friends? Maggots and grave robbers?

Marley   No, Scrooge. Ghosts. Three more will follow. Each one more terrifying than the last.

Scrooge   These ghosts, what will their names be? Nonsense, Claptrap and Humbug?

Marley   Goodbye, Scrooge. The spirit of the season will be with you.

Scrooge   I doubt it.

Marley   Oh, she will be. I hear her coming . . .

Marley *retreats from* **Scrooge**'s *room.*

An other-worldly sound grows – carols and Christmas bells backwards – heralding the arrival of the **Ghost of Christmas Past**.

Scrooge   What is that? What's happening?

The **Ghost of Christmas Past** *emerges. It is an ancient child, carrying the hope and innocence of a newborn – and the weight of all the years since the very first Christmas.*

Ghost of Christmas Past   Ebenezer Scrooge!

Its voice is eerie, old and young at the same time.

Scrooge   What are you, creature?

Ghost of Christmas Past   I am the Spirit of Christmas Past. I was a child the night of the first Christmas. I saw a messenger of peace and love born into this world. I was touched by His light: and have aged not a day since. I have lived for centuries: only to see the world turn, and turn again, away from peace, towards cruelty.

The First Ghost *moves forward and grabs* **Scrooge**'s *hand.*

Scrooge   No! What are you doing?

The awful, unsettling, discordant sound that heralded **The First Ghos***t begins again, as the years are peeled away.*

Scrooge   What's happening? Stop this!

And it all stops.

Ghost of Christmas Past   Do you recognise this place?

Scrooge *looks around him. We are in a workhouse – a grim, forbidding place.* **Scrooge***'s counting desk is gone, but the platform on which it rested is now revealed as a treadmill.*

Scrooge   Spirit, how have you done this?

Ghost of Christmas Past   Where are we, infant?

Scrooge   It looks like . . . the Union workhouse.

A **Constable** *enters, holding* **Mother** *none too gently by the arm. At* **Mother***'s side,* **Young Scrooge***. A* **Matron** *comes to meet them. As the* **Constable** *speaks to* **Scrooge***'s* **Mother***, the* **Matron** *takes from her a suitcase, then begins stripping her of rings, a necklace, her coat, her shoes.*

Scrooge   And that looks like my mother. And me! But she's been dead for years. This is impossible!

Ghost of Christmas Past   Could it be the world is not as the infant imagines? What a shock.

The **Constable** *addresses* **Scrooge***'s* **Mother***.*

Constable   On entering the workhouse, all your possessions will be forfeit. You will wear the workhouse uniform. You will walk the treadmill from six in the morning till eight at night.

Mother   I understand.

Constable   Your daughter has found service with a reputable family, but your son is still a dependent. He will be taken from you.

Mother   What? You can't.

Constable   You have thrown yourself on the charity of the state. You are not fit to raise a child.

Mother   But that's not fair!

Constable (*less official*)   It's not fair I pay my taxes to support the likes of you, but that's what the law says!

Mother   He stays with me!

Matron   Miss. The boy's last memory of his mother can be that she smiled and bid him do his best. Or he can remember you kicking and screaming as you were dragged away. Which do you think will be most reassuring to the child?

Mother   I'll go quietly.

Constable   Say your goodbyes.

Mother *sings her version of the 'Love Song'.*

Sometimes
The sun shines.
Sometimes
It rains.
When day ends,
It's night-time.
When dawn breaks,
It's day.

Sun, rain, night and day
I'll be loving you.
Sun, rain, night and day
Will you remember to love me too?

And almost before she is finished, the **Constable** *leads* **Mother** *away.*

Mother   Never forget me, Ebenezer. I'll never forget you!

Ghost of Christmas Past   You do not recall this scene?

Scrooge   Not a bit of it.

Matron   Boy, let me see your hands.

Young Scrooge *holds out his hands for inspection. He's holding a teddy bear.*

Matron   What is that?

Young Scrooge   My teddy bear. My mother gave him to me. Would you like to hold him?

She is caught off guard by the offer.

Matron   Yes, please.

Young Scrooge *gives her the teddy bear.*

Young Scrooge   He is the finest teddy bear in all the world. So my mother told me.

Matron   Yes, I'm sure he is.

The **Ghost** *looks from* **Young Scrooge** *and the* **Matron** *to* **Scrooge**.

Matron   I'm going to have to take this. You aren't allowed to keep any of your own things when you come into the workhouse. Those are the rules.

The **Matron** *is checking his hair for nits, peering in his mouth.*

Young Scrooge   Perhaps Mother will buy me another teddy.

Matron   Yes, perhaps.

Young Scrooge   And when will I see my mother again? If you don't mind me asking? Please, miss, please.

Matron *will not be able to cope if the boy's stoicism breaks. And so she snaps, before he can.*

Matron   Now that's quite enough of this nonsense! You're in the workhouse – you'll work for your living!

She pushes **Young Scrooge** *towards the treadmill.*

He tries to turn the mill. It's a huge struggle.

Young Scrooge   I can't!

Matron   Push, boy! Push or it'll be the worse for you!

The **Constable** *returns.*

Constable   What's going on?

Young Scrooge   It's too heavy, sir. Or I am too weak.
I haven't eaten since Sunday last.

Constable   Because your feckless mother was too poor to
buy bread.

Young Scrooge   Perhaps I could be allowed a mouthful
of bread now?

Constable   You'd like a handout, would you, young man?

Young Scrooge   Some bread to give me strength and then
I'll work, sir, I'll work all you like!

Constable   What humbug! Perhaps I can encourage you
another way –

The **Constable** *unbuckles his belt.*

Young Scrooge   If you would, sir.

Constable   – with my belt!

Young Scrooge   How will your belt encourage me?

Constable   Like this –

He lashes **Young Scrooge**.

Young Scrooge   Sir! Please!

Constable   Work, boy! Put some effort into it!

Terrified and in agony, **Young Scrooge** *finds the strength to turn the
treadmill.*

Constable   You see, Matron? He had the strength all along.
He just doesn't want to work, that's his problem.

The **Constable** *begins the 'Treadmill Song' – a grinding, relentless
work chant – and* **Young Scrooge** *joins in.*

Sing, sing, the treadmill song,
You're here cos you're poor,
You're here cos you're wrong,
Your life will be hell

But it won't be very long:
You're nothing! You're nothing!
You're nothing! You're nothing!

Ghost of Christmas Past   Do you remember this, Scrooge?

Scrooge   Children need a firm hand.

Constable (*to* **Young Scrooge**, *kindly*)   Any time you feel like stopping, young man, just call out – (*sudden fury*) and I'll beat you till your bones crack! I'll beat you till I break your back!

Ghost of Christmas Past   What an enlightened, rational time you live in.

Scrooge   Do you expect me to condemn the man? He is only doing his job.

The **Constable** *joins* **Young Scrooge** *for the refrain ('You're nothing, you're nothing, you're nothing, you're nothing!').*

Scrooge   I've seen enough. Let us be gone.

The First Ghost *offers his hand – and* **Scrooge** *takes it.*

The **Ghost***'s power propels them through time once again.*

We find ourselves now in a shop. The treadmill from the workhouse remains, but now it is a platform on top of which sits **Scrooge***'s desk: a simple thing, not the edifice that exists in the present day – but getting there.*

Scrooge   Ah, now this I do remember – Fezziwig the Grocer's, the place of my first employment.

Dick Wilkins *runs on and gets down to work – it's two minutes before closing time and he still has an order to get out.*

Scrooge   And Dick! My fine old friend Dick Wilkins!

Dick   A jar of capers, a side of beef, three oranges, crystallised ginger . . . where is the crystallised ginger?

From offstage a voice rumbles.

Fezziwig (*off*)   What is this?

On comes **Fezziwig**, *apparently furious.*

Fezziwig   I can't believe what I'm seeing.

Dick   It's just Mr Ricketts' order left and I'm working as fast I can, Mr Fezziwig!

Fezziwig   And you will stop this *instant*, sir!

And now **Fezziwig** *is smiling.*

Scrooge   Fezziwig! Dear old Fezziwig! Dear old bumptious, rumptious Fezziwig.

Fezziwig   We can hardly begin Christmas with the shop still open for business.

Dick   Closing the shop, sir.

Fezziwig   Festivities must begin immediately.

And **Dick** *is rushing around, attending to the – apparently – thousands of things that need doing to close for the night.*

Dick   Beginning festivities, sir.

Fezziwig   Clear space for romps and gambols and all sorts of merriment!

Dick   Clearing space, sir.

Scrooge   What a joy it would be to exchange a word with dear old Fezziwig.

Ghost of Christmas Past   Then speak.

Scrooge   But – I have aged. How do I explain my appearance?

Ghost of Christmas Past   He is but a memory. A shadow. He will see you now, as he saw you then. Speak – if to speak would bring you joy . . .

Scrooge (*tentatively*)   Mr Fezziwig, sir?

Fezziwig   Ebenezer, what is it?

Scrooge *cannot quite believe he is really speaking to his old master.*

Scrooge   It is a fine thing to see you again.

Fezziwig   See me again? You saw me not ten minutes gone. Your head must be fuzzy, to forget seeing old Fezziwig. And what clears a fuzzy head, Dick?

Dick   I'm sure I don't know, sir . . .

He knows very well!

Fezziwig   Brandy! A strong tot of brandy clears a head! So say our ancestors and I'll not ignore their wisdom, or else the country's doomed. Pour a brandy for this beleaguered boy, Dick.

Dick   Pouring the brandy, sir.

Fezziwig   And one for yourself, and one for me – this fuzziness might be contagious.

Scrooge   Oh, I can't take brandy, sir – I have the day's takings to add up, the income and outgoings to be balanced . . .

Fezziwig   Vicars and bakers work at Christmas, the rest of us take a holiday and are thankful for it. (*Shouting off.*) Mrs Fezziwig?

Mrs Fezziwig (*off*)   Coming, Mr Fezziwig!

Fezziwig   Dick, the accordion, if you please.

Dick   Acquiring the accordion, sir.

Mrs Fezziwig *comes on with a big tray of food, and* **Fezziwig** *tops up everyone's brandy.*

Fezziwig   Now – let the merriment commence!

Dick   Commencing merriment, sir.

Dick *strikes up a tune (the reel 'Sir Roger de Coverley'), and* **Fezziwig** *and* **Mrs Fezziwig** *begin to dance – a wild, whirling dance with little finesse about it.*

Fezziwig   Your turn, Ebenezer.

Scrooge   I'm not a great dancer . . .

Fezziwig   Come along, Ebenezer.

Scrooge   I have so much work still to do, sir.

Fezziwig   This is your first Christmas with us, and you will join in our festivities and rituals.

Mrs Fezziwig   It's like joining the family.

Fezziwig   It is *exactly* like that, Mrs Fezziwig – very well spoken.

Mrs Fezziwig   Thank you kindly, Mr Fezziwig.

Scrooge   I suppose I could have just one dance . . .

Fezziwig   That's the spirit!

Scrooge   What harm could it do?

But then – the 'Treadmill Song' begins.

And the **Constable** *emerges from the shadows.*

Constable   Hello hello hello, what's all this then?

Dick   What shall I play – a reel or a jig?

Constable   Is there a boy here, who means to shirk?

Scrooge   No, I'll work!

Fezziwig   Ebenezer, will you take your place?

Scrooge *rushes back to his desk and begins counting up coins.*

Scrooge   I'm working! I'm making money!

Fezziwig   But work is done for the day.

Constable   Do you need some encouragement, boy?

Scrooge   Don't beat me, please, sir.

Fezziwig   What?

Mrs Fezziwig   Husband!

Fezziwig   Of course I'm not going to beat you!

Mrs Fezziwig   Husband: leave him.

Fezziwig *turns back to his wife.*

Mrs Fezziwig   We invited him into our family. He chooses not to join. He is a grown man.

Fezziwig   Yes, I know, but –

Mrs Fezziwig   Husband! We'll have a jig, if you please.

Dick *strikes up a jig, and* **Fezziwig** *and* **Mrs Fezziwig** *begin to dance.* **Scrooge** *is still totting up his coins, putting them into bags.*

Ghost of Christmas Past   We have seen enough. We move on.

Once more they travel in time. **Fezziwig, Mrs Fezziwig** *and* **Dick** *are whirled away by their dance.*

Scrooge *is still at his desk, singing the 'Treadmill Song' to himself, unaccompanied.*

Ghost of Christmas Past   Scrooge! Do you know when we are?

Scrooge *looks up.*

Scrooge   No idea.

Ghost of Christmas Past   So few years you have lived. And so much you have lost. Do you recognise her?

Scrooge *looks where the* **Ghost** *indicates – and sees* **Belle** *approaching. Instantly he forgets his counting.*

Belle *is advancing towards him.*

Belle   You promised you'd meet me at quarter to. The clocks just rang half past.

As soon as he is speaking to **Belle**, **Scrooge** *takes on the demeanour of a much younger man.*

Scrooge   Fezziwig kept me with the usual Christmas festivities – drinking, dancing, games of blind man's bluff.

Belle   Three years you've been at Fezziwig's: never once have you joined his Christmas revels. You were working!

Scrooge   I was talking to Marley. Marley thinks I should go into business with him. Marley says you can make money simply from money – he says it's like magic!

Belle   Marley, Marley, Marley! You know, it worries me, your obsession with money.

Scrooge   Why would that worry you? It should reassure you that I am a man of excellent prospects.

Belle   A man cannot devote himself to work alone. He must find time to be a husband. And a father.

Scrooge   And I will do all those things.

Belle   So you said last year. And the year before that . . . Don't you want us to be a family?

Scrooge   But of course –

Belle   A little boy, and a little girl. Imagine it.

A boy and a girl appear – the image of **Belle** *and* **Scrooge***'s children. They are happy and joyful, playing together with a wooden hoop.*

Belle   You'd be a wonderful father.

Scrooge   Do you truly think so?

The boy rolls the hoop to **Scrooge***, and* **Scrooge** *rolls it back.*

Belle   Yes! A son, to carry on your business.

Scrooge   And . . . a daughter?

Belle   To treat like a princess and spoil rotten!

Scrooge   My children would have the best of everything, naturally!

Belle   What d'you say, then? Shall we be married in the New Year?

Scrooge   I suppose I am making a decent living . . .

Belle Is that a yes?

The 'Treadmill Song' begins.

Ben?

The **Constable** *appears. The boy and girl flee from him in fear.*

Constable Evening all.

Scrooge I can't bicker about this now –

Belle Bicker?

Scrooge I have to get back to work.

Belle What, now, at Christmas?

Constable Perhaps my belt can help settle this?

Scrooge *runs away from* **Belle** *and to his desk.*

Scrooge Without Christmas, we'd barely make a profit at all!

Constable I'll beat you till your bones crack!

Belle Ben, will you answer me?

Constable I'll beat you till I break your back!

Belle If you will not marry me, Ben, then we should not see each other again.

Scrooge *looks up from his desk.*

Scrooge What?

Belle (*cutting across him*) You love money more than you ever could me.

Scrooge Such genteel complaints!

Belle I never dreamed I would hear you speak to me with such contempt.

Constable You are nothing, boy. You've got nothing, so you are nothing.

Scrooge *turns on* **Belle** *in a fury.*

Scrooge   Fine. If that's the way you want it – we're finished. Now if you would care to return my engagement ring.

Belle   My ring? But this was a gift.

Scrooge   It was a prelude to marriage.

Belle   I beg you, let me keep it.

Scrooge   Oh, you'd love to hang on to that. Real diamonds, and all gold, not just plate.

Belle   Not for the money! As a keepsake. In memory of the love we had between us. Don't rob me of that. For pity's sake, Mr Scrooge –

Scrooge   What did you call me?

Belle   For pity's sake, Ben –

Scrooge   Give me what you owe me!

Belle *takes off the ring and hands it to* **Scrooge**. *She flees.*

Ghost of Christmas Past   Do you see, Scrooge?

Scrooge   See what?

Ghost of Christmas Past   I call you infant, because you are an infant. You are still that boy on the treadmill, stripped of everything for the want of money.

Scrooge   No one will ever order me around. No one will take my things. No one will ever beat me again. And all because I am rich.

Ghost of Christmas Past   But money is all you do have. Money is your master now, just as it was when you were a boy.

Scrooge   Is that the lesson I'm supposed to learn?

Ghost of Christmas Past   What other lesson is there?

Song: 'The System Works'.

I was born to a family
Of layabouts, and beggars.
My life promised nothing

But poverty, and pain.
I was taken from my mother –
A deadbeat, a loser –
As she wept her goodbyes,
I was born again.

The system that made me
Was stone bed, cold food.
The system that made me
Was harsh words, hard hearts.
The system that made me
Was belts and beatings.
The system that made me
Gave me a brand-new start.

An inmate at the workhouse –
A cog in the system –
My days were filled with
Labour and strain.
All this was thanks to
My family's poverty.
I resolved that I
Would never be poor again.

The system that made me
Was stone bed, cold food . . . (*etc.*)

And now, look at me –
A rich man, the richest! –
My days are blessed with
Profit and gain.
So you may criticise
The system that made me.
My mind is satisfied
I'd live it all again.

The system that made me
Was stone bed, cold food.
The system that made me
Was harsh words, hard hearts.
The system that made me
Was belts and beatings.

The system that made me
Gave me a brand-new start –
Cos the system works.
The system works.
The system works.
The system works.

Ghost of Christmas Past   And you have lost nothing, by devoting your life to money?

Scrooge   Like what?

Ghost of Christmas Past   Like love? For your fellow man . . . or woman.

Scrooge   Love? What drivel! What piffle! What humbug!

Ghost of Christmas Past   Really?

The **Ghost** *advances on* **Scrooge**.

Scrooge   What are you doing? Get off me!

Ghost of Christmas Past   What is this we find here? Around your neck?

Scrooge   I have no idea.

Ghost of Christmas Past   It is the engagement ring you took back from Belle.

Scrooge   I always carry gold about my person – what if there were a revolution, and I was forced to flee to the Americas?

Ghost of Christmas Past   What drivel. What piffle.

Scrooge   I had forgotten it was there.

Ghost of Christmas Past   You forgot you put her ring on a chain? And forgot you placed it round your neck? And forgot it was next to your very heart? What humbug!

Scrooge   Yes, all right. You find me guilty of one small sentimentality: I kept her ring. But worry not, Spirit, I will learn your lesson.

Ghost of Christmas Past   I am relieved to hear that!

Scrooge   Boxing Day, when the jewellers open, I'll swap this little trinket for honest coin. Now: is there anything else you wish to show me, or are we quite finished?

Ghost of Christmas Past   One last thing. Then I will be gone.

Scrooge   Thank goodness!

He offers his hand, this time. **The First Ghost** *takes it.*

We travel – to **Scrooge***'s counting house.*

Scrooge   Well, of course I recognise this place.

Ghost of Christmas Past   The infant knows where we are – does he know when?

Scrooge   Christmas, no doubt.

Ghost of Christmas Past   But which Christmas?

A couple of **Workmen** *come on with the piece which transforms* **Scrooge***'s desk into the grand edifice that exists in the present day.*

Workman   Where d'you want this, guv?

Scrooge *indicates the desk.*

Scrooge   Over there. And be careful! (*To the* **Ghost**.) Yes, I remember. It's Christmas, seven years ago.

Ghost of Christmas Past   And why do you think I have brought you to this moment?

Scrooge   This is the very first year *The Times* put me top of the Rich List.

He is climbing up onto his desk.

Ghost of Christmas Past   That is true, but that is not why we have come.

Scrooge   What else, then? Seven years ago, Christmas Eve . . .

He can't think of anything.

Everything was perfectly normal.

Ghost of Christmas Past   Everything?

Scrooge *realises.*

Scrooge   Oh.

Ghost of Christmas Past   Christmas Eve. Seven years ago. Jacob Marley fell to cholera.

And we see **Marley**, *lying abed.*

Ghost of Christmas Past   A fever burning hotter and higher. Jacob Marley, your friend, your partner, lay dying.

Marley   Help me. Help me, someone!

Ghost of Christmas Past   And you – going about your business.

Marley   Please, I'm frightened.

Ghost of Christmas Past   And you – making money.

Scrooge   What else was I supposed to do? I may be rich, but riches cannot remedy cholera!

Marley   Just someone to hold my hand . . .

He raises a hand towards **Scrooge**.

Ghost of Christmas Past   *Enough!* I am done with you, Ebenezer Scrooge.

And with that, the **Ghost** *and* **Marley** *are gone.* **Scrooge** *is left alone.*

Scrooge   I carried on, business as usual – that's what Marley would have wanted! Spirit, d'you hear me?

There's no response.

So you've gone then, have you? I've won?

He listens for answer – there is none. He forces himself to calm.

He waits.

Come on, spirit number two. I'm ready for anything, from pitch-and-toss to manslaughter!

The wind howls outside. **Scrooge** *is getting a bit jumpy.*

Do not torment me, spirit – this waiting is worst of all!

How chilling, how ghastly, how terrifying can this next spirit be?

And then – from the back of the auditorium –

Ghost of Christmas Present   Hiya! Hiya everybody!

This **Ghost** *is a giant figure, a big, camp Welsh bear of a man, dressed in a red coat lined with fur.*

Ghost of Christmas Present   Yes, it's me – Christmas has come, happy days are here, the party starts if not right now this second then right now in a minute, for definite.

Scrooge   What abomination is this?

The **Ghost** *moves down the auditorium, greeting people as he passes, handing out party hats.*

Ghost of Christmas Present   Apparently there is someone around who doesn't like Christmas? Somebody called Scrooge? I'm looking for Ebenezer Scrooge, anybody know who this Ebenezer Scrooge feller is?

He picks someone from the audience.

Is it you?

And someone else.

Is it you? Love your hair, by the way.

And someone else.

Is it you then? No? So where is he? Where is this Scrooge?

Scrooge   Sir Ghost. I fear I may be the Scrooge you are looking for.

Ghost of Christmas Present   You're Scrooge, are you? Well, Benny boy, I gotta say you look about as much fun as a wet weekend in Port Talbot.

Scrooge   We are not intimates, sir, kindly refrain from using my Christian name.

Ghost of Christmas Present   Come again?

Scrooge   Stop calling me Ben!

Ghost of Christmas Present   Don't get your britches backwards! All right, *Mr* Scrooge, let me introduce myself. I am the Spirit of Christmas Present. I'm going to show you how much fun you miss out every Christmas by being a grumpy old misery guts.

Scrooge   I believe Christmas to be an irrational waste of time and effort.

Ghost of Christmas Present   What? Christmas is cowin' lush, mun.

Scrooge   I have a song which expounds my argument admirably.

He clears his throat, preparatory to singing –

Ghost of Christmas Present   Yeah, we've all heard your miserable dirge. Now it's time for my big number.

*The **Ghost**'s riposte to **Scrooge**.*

Song: 'Yeah! Christmas! Cowin' Lush!'

> Christmas comes but once a year,
> And once is not enough
> For goodwill, happiness and cheer
> And all that lovely stuff.
> I say it's a time when hate
> Is put aside for reason
> That is why we must abide
> By the spirit of the Christmas season.
>
> You may not like your mother,
> You may hate your dear old dad,
> At Christmas you invite them round
> And it makes you feel so glad.
> You remember how they cared for you

When you were just a little 'un
You pack them off on Boxing Day –
By New Year's Eve you miss them.

Christmas comes but once a year,
And once is not enough
For goodwill, happiness and cheer
And all that lovely stuff.
I say it's a time when hate
Is put aside for reason,
That is why we must abide
By the spirit of the Christmas season.

You may not have a penny
You may scrimp and dress in rags.
At Christmas you make party hats
From torn up-paper bags.
You give up everything you can
So you can give to others,
And people who were strange
Feel like your sisters and your brothers.

Christmas comes but once a year,
And once is not enough
For goodwill, happiness and cheer
And all that lovely stuff.
I say it's a time when hate
Is put aside for reason,
That is why we must abide
By the spirit of the Christmas season.

As the song is performed, **The Second Ghost** *distributes gifts, produces mistletoe and snatches kisses, hands letters from home to a soldier – generally makes everyone happy.*

Scrooge   Sir Ghost, I find you frivolous, and ridiculous. Please depart this instant.

Ghost of Christmas Present   You say Christmas is all humbug, but look how it cheers everybody up.

Scrooge   I see people pretending to kindness and cheer for this one day of the year, because they feel they must.

Ghost of Christmas Present   Oh, you are hard work, I'll give you that. On we go then. Let's see some sights closer to home. Or closer to work, for you.

They travel – in space, but not in time.

Scrooge   Where are we? What district is this?

Ghost of Christmas Present   This, my friend, is Camden.

Scrooge   Camden? I've heard rumour of its depravity, but never before trodden its squalid byways.

Ghost of Christmas Present (*indicating the house*)   You don't know who lives here?

Scrooge   Should I?

Ghost of Christmas Present   Bob Cratchit.

Scrooge   Bob Cratchit my clerk?

Ghost of Christmas Present   No, Bob Cratchit the Prince of Wales. Of course Bob Cratchit your clerk.

Scrooge   Bob Cratchit lives here? In this miserable shack?

Ghost of Christmas Present   It's all he can afford – apparently his boss is a right old miser . . .

Scrooge   I pay the going rate. Almost.

Ghost of Christmas Present   It may be a miserable shack – shall we see if it makes for a miserable home?

*Inside **Bob Cratchit***'s house, **Mrs Cratchit** and **Martha Cratchit**.

Mrs Cratchit   They're coming!

Martha Cratchit   I'll hide!

Bob Cratchit and **Peter Cratchit** *enter,* **Bob** *carrying* **Tiny Tim** *on his shoulders.*

Bob Cratchit   Where's Martha?

Mrs Cratchit   Martha? Not coming.

Bob Cratchit   Not coming?

Tiny Tim   Not coming? On Christmas Day?

Mrs Cratchit   They offered her three whole shillings if she'd stay and serve Christmas dinner!

Bob Cratchit   What? Away from the family? At Christmas?

Ghost of Christmas Present (*to* **Scrooge**)   You look confused.

Scrooge   Not having his daughter near seems . . . to pain him, almost.

Ghost of Christmas Present   Yeah. Funny that, isn't it?

Bob Cratchit   Right – I'm going up to the manor and telling them, they can serve dinner for themselves on this day if no other.

Martha *reveals herself.*

Martha Cratchit   Father, I'm here!

Bob Cratchit   Oh, you had me good and proper, Martha Cratchit.

He hugs his daughter.

Martha Cratchit   As if I'd stay away at Christmas . . .

Mrs Cratchit   And how was Tim, at church?

Bob Cratchit   Good as gold. Walked all the way there, by himself.

Martha Cratchit   Our Tim's getting stronger every day, isn't he?

Bob Cratchit   I've never seen a boy so healthy and strong!

Peter Cratchit (*to* **Tim**)   Soon you'll be throwing those crutches away!

Tiny Tim   I hope so, brother.

Bob Cratchit   Why waste them? We can use them as firewood!

The **Cratchits** *busy themselves laying the table for Christmas dinner.*

Ghost of Christmas Present   Again, Scrooge, I see there is something that befuddles you.

Scrooge   The boy is not healthy, nor strong – why do they lie?

Ghost of Christmas Present   Perhaps they lie to give him hope.

Scrooge   False hope, then.

Ghost of Christmas Present   Perhaps they lie, because they can't bear to tell the truth.

Scrooge   And what is the truth? What will happen to Tiny Tim?

Ghost of Christmas Present   He needs good food and plenty of it. He needs to see the doctor, and he needs medicine. But all those things cost money.

Bob Cratchit   And now – the goose!

Mrs Cratchit *brings in a goose. It is a tiny thing.*

Martha Cratchit   What a bird!

Scrooge   Goose! It's a sparrow at best!

Bob Cratchit   But before we tuck in – Tim?

Tiny Tim   For what we are about to receive, may the Lord make us truly thankful.

All the Cratchits   Amen.

The **Cratchits** *busy themselves passing microscopic portions of vegetables,* **Bob Cratchit** *carving the meat. They sing the meal's praises – 'Best roast potatoes we've had, well, since last Christmas', and so on, despite each having only a tiny amount of food, ideally on massively oversized plates.*

Scrooge   They are pleased enough with this meagre feast.

Ghost of Christmas Present   No, Scrooge. They are pleased to be close to the ones they love most. Pleased to be sharing. Pleased to be together, at Christmas.

Bob Cratchit   Well, we seem to have scoffed the lot!

Mrs Cratchit   Yes, I'm sorry there wasn't / more.

Martha Cratchit (*cutting across*)   We're such greedy guts we ate all that mountain of food! We better have a rest before pudding.

Bob Cratchit   Let's drink a toast. A merry Christmas to us, my dears. God bless us.

Tiny Tim   God bless us, every one.

Bob Cratchit   And a toast to the founder of our feast – Mr Ebenezer Scrooge.

Scrooge   What's this? They toast me?

Peter Cratchit   The founder of the feast?

Mrs Cratchit   I wish he was here, I'd give him a piece of my mind to feast upon!

Bob Cratchit   My dear! Christmas Day!

Mrs Cratchit   I'll drink Scrooge's health, for your sake and for Christmas Day, but not for his. Long life to him, a merry Christmas and a happy New Year. He'll be very merry and happy, I have no doubt.

Bob Cratchit *raises his glass. The others follow.*

All the Cratchits   Mr Scrooge.

Bob *and* **Mrs Cratchit** *are painfully aware the mood has dipped.*

Bob Cratchit   What about a game?

Mrs Cratchit   Yes! What shall we play?

Tiny Tim   The Guessing Game!

Martha Cratchit   Oh, I've got something, let me go first.

Mrs Cratchit   Is it animal?

Martha Cratchit   No.

Bob Cratchit   Is it vegetable?

Martha Cratchit   No.

Peter Cratchit   Mineral.

Martha Cratchit   Yes!

Bob Cratchit   Is it gold?

Martha Cratchit   It is . . . next to gold, but not gold.

Mrs Cratchit   Diamonds?

Martha Cratchit   It loves diamonds, but is not diamonds.

Mrs Cratchit (*somewhat aside*)   You said it was a mineral, how can a mineral / love anything –

Tiny Tim (*over* **Mrs Cratchit**)   Is it rubies?

Martha Cratchit   No!

Peter Cratchit   Oh well then, we give up.

Martha Cratchit   It's Scrooge!

Bob, **Mrs** *and* **Peter Cratchit** *speak all at once* –

Bob Cratchit   What?

Mrs Cratchit   I said animal, you said no!

Peter Cratchit   How is Scrooge a mineral?

Martha Cratchit   His heart is stone. His head is stone. He is stone through and through!

Tiny Tim   He is, too!

Bob Cratchit   Well . . . that's a little bit mean, but –

Mrs Cratchit   Mean but true!

Martha Cratchit   Not as mean as the man himself!

Mrs Cratchit   Who would've thought, Ebenezer Scrooge would give us a smile, on Christmas Day . . .

Peter Cratchit   Probably the only thing he's given to anyone all year!

And now they are smiling and happy in each other's company again.

Ghost of Christmas Present   You see, Scrooge? On Christmas Day, even a killjoy like you brings happiness. Now, will you admit how brilliant Christmas is? Will you cheer up and be a bit nicer?

Scrooge   Yes, I could raise Bob's pay. But what if, through my extravagance, I go bankrupt? If there are not lenders to extend credit, all industry halts with a grinding crunch.

Ghost of Christmas Present   It's not the pittance you pay your clerk that is extravagant, Scrooge. It's the fortune you stack up for yourself −

Scrooge   The Cratchits are poor. But what you have also demonstrated is that their . . . 'love' − their 'warmth' − their 'human kindness' − more than compensates for their poverty. They are perfectly fine, in their own grubby little way. What you have shown me is that − the system works, the system works, the system works.

Ghost of Christmas Present   You are too much, boy − that's it, it is over between me and you . . .

Scrooge   Although . . . perhaps you have shown me something else. Something I had missed, and have been missing.

Ghost of Christmas Present   And what might that be?

Scrooge   This . . . warmth. You are right. I have none in my life.

*The **Ghost** flings open his arms.*

Ghost of Christmas Present   D'you want a Christmas cuddle, make it better?

Scrooge   Don't you dare!

Ghost of Christmas Present   All right, don't get your knickerbockers knotted.

Scrooge   Am I loved by anyone?

Ghost of Christmas Present   There is someone who feels . . . shall we say? . . . warmth for you, at least.

Scrooge   Who?

Ghost of Christmas Present   Look to your heart, Scrooge.

Scrooge   My heart?

Scrooge *places a hand on his breast.*

Feels something.

Takes out the chain which carries **Belle***'s ring.*

And **Belle** *appears, walking through.*

Scrooge   Belle still loves me?

Ghost of Christmas Present   Yeah . . . I don't know if love is *quite* the word I'd use . . .

Scrooge   Can I speak to her?

Ghost of Christmas Present   This is the present. She is no shadow. She's real.

Scrooge *approaches her.*

Scrooge   Belle?

She turns.

Belle   I'm afraid you have the advantage of me, sir.

Scrooge   Oh no, Belle. It is the other way around.

Belle   Ben? Ben Scrooge? I don't believe it.

She is dumbstruck. **Scrooge** *takes this as a good sign.*

Scrooge   I can scarcely believe it myself, Belle, but it is wondrous / to see you again –

Belle (*cutting in*)   I don't believe you would dare speak to me, you rogue –

She slaps him.

You wretch –

And again!

You good-for-nothing!

And once more for good measure. **Scrooge** *retreats.*

Scrooge   You said she still loved me!

Ghost of Christmas Present   She still does, probably. Somewhere very deep down . . .

Scrooge *approaches* **Belle** *again. Not too close this time.*

Belle   I'm warning you . . .

Scrooge   Please hear me out and then I swear I'll never trouble you again. I have become the richest man in all the world.

Belle   Yes, I know.

Scrooge   You do?

Belle   Everyone knows. Top of *The Times* Rich List for six years running.

He's flattered she knows this –

Scrooge   Seven, actually.

– but dismisses it.

But I am miserable. Because for all my money, I have no love in my life.

Belle   And whose fault is that?

Scrooge   Mine, and mine alone. I had love. I abandoned it, when I abandoned you.

Belle   Can this be Ben Scrooge? Admitting he was wrong?

Scrooge   There's no ring on your finger. You haven't married?

Belle   Once bitten, twice shy. You put me off love for good, Scrooge.

Scrooge   Then you might be free to have dinner with me?

Belle   Dinner? With you?

Ghost of Christmas Present   Scrooge! What day is it?

Scrooge   December the twenty-fifth.

Ghost of Christmas Present   And that is −

Scrooge *doesn't know.*

He remembers!

Scrooge   Of course! (*Turning back to* **Belle**.) I do not deserve forgiveness. But in honour of the warmth, and kindness, and generosity of Christmas − I beg you.

Belle   It is odd to hear you speak approvingly of kindness, and warmth.

Scrooge   Perhaps I have changed.

Ghost of Christmas Present   You hear that? He's changed.

All thanks to a great big lovely **Ghost**.

Belle   This is ridiculous: I cannot dine with you. My sister is ill. I must be her nurse.

Scrooge   If she's ill, why don't you call a doctor?

Belle   We are poor, Ben. We cannot afford a doctor. My sister is sick and there is nothing I can do − apart from sit at her side, as she weakens and dies.

Scrooge   Well − why didn't you say!

He fumbles around and pulls out a note.

Five pounds cover it?

Belle   This will save my sister's life!

She kisses him on the cheek.

Ghost of Christmas Present   Do you see that?

Scrooge   I do.

Ghost of Christmas Present   See the joy on her face?

Scrooge   I do.

Ghost of Christmas Present   And don't you feel all
warm inside?

Scrooge   Do you know – I think I might.

Belle (*still incredulous at the note in her hands*)   Ben, you have no
idea how much this means to me.

Scrooge   Belle, I remember the day we parted . . . as if
I had lived through those events only minutes ago. Look –

He gets out the ring from around his neck.

Belle   My engagement ring! You said you were going to
sell it.

Scrooge   I never could. I put it on a chain. And placed it
round my neck. And kept it next to my very heart.

Scrooge *drops to one knee, takes* **Belle***'s hand.*

Belle   What are you doing?

Ghost of Christmas Present   Oh. My. GOD. Everyone,
you've got to see this!

*People rush onstage – cries of 'Scrooge – getting married?' 'Scrooge – in
love?' 'I don't believe it!'*

Scrooge *sings his version of the 'Love Song'.*

Sometimes
The sun shines.
Sometimes
It rains.
When day ends,

It's night-time.
When dawn breaks,
It's day.

Sun, rain, night and day
Now I remember that I love you.
Sun, rain, night and day
Could you try to love me too?

Ghost of Christmas Present   I'm gonna have to buy a new hat!

Scrooge   Belle – will you marry me?

Ghost of Christmas Present   Will Belle forgive the man who broke her heart? Or will she punch him in the gob and send him on his way? Tough luck, we're not gonna tell you just yet! We're gonna have a little interval, and you can go and argue about what's gonna happen, and then come back and see how it all works out. Oh, and if anybody's going to the little kiosk, can you get me an orangeade? I'm parched, I am.

Act Two

As we were.

Ghost of Christmas Present Ladies and gentlemen, my work is almost done. Once Scrooge was a grumpy old misery guts, now he's embraced warmth and kindness and humanity, and he's asked the one girl he ever loved to marry him. What's she going to say? Yes? No? Let's see.

Belle You truly wish to marry me?

Scrooge More than anything.

Belle Then my answer is – yes, and very gladly.

Scrooge *embraces her. The gathered onlookers applaud.*

Scrooge I haven't been so happy since I made my first million!

Belle Ben – to have you back, after all these years! I thought I would be lonely till the day I died. It's a miracle.

Scrooge A Christmas miracle.

Ghost of Christmas Present I can't possibly take all the credit – oh, go on then, yes I can.

On comes the **Constable***, leading the* **Match Girl** *by the arm.*

Constable Scrooge! Ebenezer Scrooge!

Scrooge What! I've done nothing wrong!

Constable This young lady owes you money.

Scrooge Ah yes . . .

Constable I have served a bankruptcy notice at your request – she wishes to plead her case with you directly.

Match Girl Please, Mr Scrooge, you can't throw me in jail.

Scrooge I can, in fact: if you care to examine the contract.

He unrolls the long contract he had the **Match Girl** *sign right at the beginning of the story.*

Scrooge   And there, that's your little circle, isn't it?

Match Girl   Yes.

Scrooge   Like the sun, which you love.

Match Girl   That's right, sir, for its / warmth –

Scrooge (*interrupting*)   So you took my shilling and agreed to pay me a penny a day for the next six months. And if you don't pay – I get everything you own! And you go to prison!

Match Girl   But without me, my children will die.

Scrooge   Yes, probably. But you can't really afford to feed them, can you? Best let the winter finish them off. At least that'll be quick.

Match Girl   Show some pity!

Scrooge   Show me my penny.

Belle   Ben?

Scrooge   Yes, angel of my heart?

Belle   What exactly are you doing?

Scrooge   Just a spot of business.

Belle   You mean to put this girl in prison?

Scrooge   All the other moneylenders are doing it, I have to compete.

Belle   You could show some mercy!

Scrooge   I see. (*He considers this.*) But why? Do you know how much I'll make if I sell her belongings? Maybe a whole pound! I put in a shilling – I get out a pound! That's a thousand per cent profit!

Belle   I thought you had changed.

Scrooge   Of course I've changed! Before I cared for only money. Now I understand that a life worth living is full of love.

Belle   Is it out of love that you will put this girl in jail? Out of love you'll let her children die?

Scrooge   But – I don't love her. I couldn't care less about her. I love you.

Belle   Then for my sake, spare her.

Scrooge   She owes me money!

Belle   She owes you a penny! If you lose a penny – so what?

Constable   Oh dear . . .

Scrooge   But that's how it starts! You lose a penny, then a shilling, then a pound –

Constable   Next thing you know, you're in the workhouse!

Scrooge   Stripped of everything you have –

Constable   – being whipped –

Scrooge   – and beaten –

Constable   – and broken –

Scrooge   – and crushed –

Constable   – and even if you get out you never get out really because you know in your heart you are nothing.

Scrooge   So no, I will not 'spare her', as if she were some mischievous child!

Belle   You're the one who's sending people to the workhouse.

Scrooge   It's not my fault if they are greedy and lazy and feckless – and poor!

Belle   For pity's sake . . .

Match Girl   Please, sir? Please, it's just – it's Christmas. There's no one on the streets buying matches. Just give me a chance, and you'll get your money. Give me a day's grace and I'll work, sir, I'll work all you like!

Scrooge *is in agony – he's swayed by the two women pleading with him, but this goes against all his instincts . . .*

. . . and the **Constable** *begins to sing the 'Treadmill Song'.*

Scrooge   No! No, enough. You –

He's pointing at the **Constable**.

Scrooge   Take her to jail, this instant.

The **Constable** *drags the* **Match Girl** *away.*

Belle   Ben, no!

Scrooge   The matter is settled, I don't want to hear any further prattling.

Belle   As you wish.

She takes off her engagement ring, and offers it back to **Scrooge**.

Scrooge   What's this?

Belle   I cannot marry a man who would throw a family on to the streets.

Scrooge   I thought you loved me.

Belle   I cannot stand by such cruelty.

She makes, somewhat deliberately, to leave.

Scrooge   Belle.

She turns straight away and runs back to him, full of hope.

Belle   Say you'll change your mind. Say you'll forgive that poor girl and we can be together.

Scrooge   I'll have my five pounds back, if you please.

Belle   What?

Scrooge   The five pounds I gave you, for your sister.

Belle   But without a doctor, she will die.

Scrooge   Yes. Well. Overpopulation is the scourge of the Empire. High time we thinned out / the herd –

Before **Scrooge** *can finish his speech,* **Belle** *throws the five-pound note to the ground and retreats.*

Belle *sings her version of the 'Love Song'.*

> Sometimes
> The sun shines.
> Sometimes
> It rains.
> When day ends,
> It's night-time.
> When dawn breaks,
> It's day.
>
> Sun, rain, night and day
> Love's what saw me through.
> Sun, rain, night and day
> Love is just a word to you.

As she sings, **Scrooge** *goes over to the note.*

Picks it up. Smoothes it out.

Scrooge   And before you start, spirit – yes, I have learned something from all this.

Ghost of Christmas Present   Really?

Scrooge   I've learned that I was right all along. Money is all that matters. Because money you can trust. Money never lies to you. Money never lets you down.

Ghost of Christmas Present   I'd love to stay and argue this all night, but honest to God, I haven't got the strength. Merry Christmas to you, Mr Scrooge.

Scrooge   Good day to you, sir.

With no **Ghost** *to make a show of belligerence to,* **Scrooge** *is distraught.*

He pulls himself together, starts skipping around like a boxer, punching and jabbing at the air.

Scrooge   He's faced two terrible opponents already tonight.

His pretence fails. He stands, heartbroken for a second.

Then pulls himself together once more, begins skipping and jabbing again.

Two hauntings down, one to go. If I were a betting man, I'd lay down a pound to say I'll see off this next ghost as I did the others. I won't, of course – betting is a fool's game, the bookmaker always wins in the end . . . Hmm. Maybe that's a thought for the New Year. Bookmaking. But should a banker become a gambler? Is that seemly? Is it safe? It's bound to be lucrative – so who cares!

Ghost of Christmas Future   SCROOOOOGE!!

This **Ghost** *is a dark figure with an icy voice. The cockiness drains out of* **Scrooge** *in an instant – he ducks to hide.*

Ghost of Christmas Future   Ebenezer Scrooge!

Scrooge *raises his hand, like a pupil answering to the register.*

Scrooge   Here, sir.

Ghost of Christmas Future   Do you know me?

Scrooge   I'd been given to expect a spirit of Christmas.

Ghost of Christmas Future   And here I am.

Scrooge   You are a spirit of Christmas?

Ghost of Christmas Future   Do you doubt me?

Scrooge   Where's the holly? Where's the ivy? Where's the peace and goodwill and all that humbug?

Ghost of Christmas Future   I am the Spirit of Christmas Yet to Come.

Scrooge   I don't understand.

Ghost of Christmas Future   In the Christmases that are to come for you, there is little goodwill, or peace. Let me show you.

Scrooge   D'you know, I don't think I'll bother.

Ghost of Christmas Future   TAKE MY HAND!

They begin to travel. Moving as spookily as the **Ghost of Christmas Past** *did into what had gone before − but now we're headed to the future.*

Instantly, there's something up with **Scrooge**.

Scrooge   I don't feel right.

Ghost of Christmas Future   You feel as you should.

Scrooge   Everything hurts, everything's heavy.

Ghost of Christmas Future   The load you will have to bear is heavy indeed.

Scrooge   I need to sit down.

Ghost of Christmas Future   Sit, rest your weary bones.

Scrooge *slumps to the floor.*

Scrooge   Oh, that's much better.

Ghost of Christmas Future   Enjoy it, Ebenezer. For you will never rise again.

Scrooge   What? I can rise whenever I want −

He tries − and he can't.

What's this? I can't get up. My arms − I'm too weak.

Ghost of Christmas Future   Old age does not come alone, Scrooge. It arrives with friends: frailty and weakness chief among them.

Scrooge   How do I eat? How do I survive?

Ghost of Christmas Future   Others have family who might care for them as they grow older. Not you.

Scrooge   Then what do I do?

Ghost of Christmas Future   Others have friends who might take them in. Not you.

Scrooge   What are you saying? Is this how it all ends? Me, stuck here, starving to death?

Ghost of Christmas Future   Perhaps . . .

Scrooge *looks at the third* **Ghost**. *And figures something out.*

Scrooge   I don't need family or friends. And you know why, spirit? Because I've got money! What matter if no one cares about me? I can pay them to care! (*Shouts to off.*) Housekeeper! Get in here, right now!

The **Housekeeper** *enters. She's carrying a bowl of gruel and a bib.*

Housekeeper   Come along now, Mr Scrooge, let's be having you.

Scrooge (*to the third* **Ghost**)   No matter what happens, I'll be fine, Spirit. Thanks to all my money! (*To the* **Housekeeper**.) You, help me to my chair.

Housekeeper   As you please, sir.

She wheels over a bath chair, and begins to lift **Scrooge** *into it.*

Scrooge   What are you doing? I mean up there, at my desk.

Housekeeper   You can't get up there, sir, you haven't the strength.

Scrooge   I need to keep an eye on the accounts.

Housekeeper   What accounts?

Scrooge   The accounts of my business, idiot female.

Housekeeper   Your memory is getting worse, Mr Scrooge. Have you forgotten, you loaned all that money to people who couldn't pay it back? So they didn't pay it back? And your business collapsed?

Scrooge   Am I no longer the richest man in the world?

Housekeeper   Not to worry, you're still richer than anyone else I know.

Scrooge   From richest man in the world, to richest acquaintance of a charlady! How I am fallen!

Housekeeper   Getting by on the last ten million must be a trial indeed . . .

The **Housekeeper** *puts the bib, none too gently, around* **Scrooge***'s neck.*

Scrooge   What's this? What assault! What indignity!

Housekeeper   Open wide – the choo-choo train is coming down the track!

She shovels up a spoonful of gruel, and shoves it towards his mouth.

Scrooge   What are you doing, woman?

Housekeeper   Trying to give you your supper.

Scrooge   I'll eat when I'm ready, not according to your convenience.

The clock chimes eight. The **Housekeeper***'s demeanour shifts instantly – the forced jollity is gone, replaced by weariness and cynicism.*

Housekeeper   As you please.

She puts down the bowl, picks up her coat and scarf.

Scrooge   What are you doing?

Housekeeper   Eight o'clock. I'm off duty.

She busies herself making final preparations to leave – putting things where they should be, snuffing out unnecessary candles and, in particular, moving a bucket from some discreet location and putting it at the foot of **Scrooge***'s chair.*

Scrooge   And you're just going? And leaving me?

Housekeeper   I work eight till eight, sir. Those are the hours you pay me.

Scrooge   I am to be abandoned till eight o'clock tomorrow morning?

Housekeeper   Actually, I won't be in tomorrow, at all.

Scrooge   What?

Housekeeper   Tomorrow is Christmas. I am allowed a
day's holiday.

Scrooge   You'll leave me, all on my own?

Housekeeper   That is the contract we signed, Mr Scrooge.

And she produces a long, unfurling contract – just like the one **Scrooge**
used with the **Match Girl.**

Housekeeper   It's all in the small print.

Scrooge   What if I need a wee?

Housekeeper   The bucket is at your feet.

Scrooge   You can't leave me! Not at Christmas!

Housekeeper   Mr Scrooge – it is well known that you do
not keep Christmas. Good day.

She starts to leave.

Scrooge   You villain! Consider your contract terminated!
I never want to see you again!

Housekeeper   As you please, Mr Scrooge.

She exits.

Ghost of Christmas Future   Are you sure that was wise?

Scrooge   What? I can always get another housekeeper. And
she was useless.

Ghost of Christmas Future   And *how* will you get
another housekeeper?

Scrooge   I'll just go to the markets and hire a girl, it's
perfectly simple . . .

Ghost of Christmas Future   How will you reach the
market, Scrooge – when you cannot walk?

Scrooge   It's Christmas! My nephew turns up every year,
desperate I grace his dreary dinner.

Strolling nearby are **Fred**, **Scrooge**'s *nephew,* and **Fred's Wife**.

Scrooge   Fred! Fred my dear boy!

Fred's Wife   Did you hear that?

Fred   I heard nothing.

He clearly did hear.

Fred's Wife   I'm sure I heard your Uncle Scrooge, calling you by name.

Scrooge   You did, excellent girl!

Fred   A man called Scrooge lives nearby: I am no nephew to him, he is no uncle to me. And that is his choice, not mine.

Fred's Wife   But at Christmas, Fred – for pity's sake.

Fred   I'll show him as much pity as he shows anyone else. Which is to say – none at all.

He leads his wife away.

Ghost of Christmas Future   Scrooge: your nephew has not called for many years. Because you told him not to.

Scrooge   Ah! There is yet one man! (*Shouting*) Bob! Bob Cratchit, assist me!

Ghost of Christmas Future   You think Bob Cratchit will come to your rescue?

Scrooge   Yes, yes, because – it was your ghostly brother, spirit, that showed me, good old Bob Cratchit raising a glass and toasting me, the founder of the feast. (*Shouting*) Bob! Bob Cratchit, I need you! (*To the third* **Ghost**.) Bob knows what little he has, all comes from Scrooge.

Ghost of Christmas Future   We'll see, shall we?

Scrooge   Yes, we will see –

Bob Cratchit *enters. Dressed all in black, a hat on his head.*

Scrooge   And here he is!

Bob Cratchit   You bellowed, Mr Scrooge?

Scrooge   Yes, and you dawdled, Mr Cratchit. A bit of haste might not be out of place when your master calls.

Bob Cratchit   You paid my wages, sir, such as they were: I don't recall that you were ever my master.

Scrooge   Quibble on your own time, Mr Cratchit: now, thanks to being let down by my useless ex-housekeeper, I'm going to need you to come here tomorrow and look after me.

Bob Cratchit   Tomorrow?

Scrooge   Yes, tomorrow, Christmas Day. It'll just be feeding me, washing me, cleaning this place, doing my laundry, entertaining me with readings or perhaps a song – oh, and you'll need to find a new housekeeper before business opens again on Boxing Day.

Bob Cratchit   I can't, sir.

Scrooge   You can't? What babble! What bombast! What humbug!

Bob Cratchit   Tomorrow is my son's funeral.

Scrooge   I beg your pardon?

Bob Cratchit   My son, sir. Tim. Tiny Tim, we used to call him. I did mention to you that he was ill, sir. And then I mentioned to you that he was dreadful ill, sir.

And then I mentioned to you that he had died.

Perhaps you had forgotten – you are a very busy man, I know, with . . . investments to be thinking about. I can think of nothing else but my son.

Scrooge   I don't know what to say.

Bob Cratchit   Others have offered their sympathy. Told me how sorry they are. Asked if there is anything they can do to help. But you, Mr Scrooge, do not know what to say. I am not surprised. (*Beat.*) I will take my leave of you now.

And **Bob Cratchit** *is gone.*

Ghost of Christmas Future   You look shocked, Scrooge?

Scrooge's *shock has been genuine. But now he covers it up.*

Scrooge   It's not my fault the boy died! I didn't make him sick.

Ghost of Christmas Future   But neither did you make him strong. A few shillings more, better food, a warm bed, a doctor when he needed one. Such simple things. You could have given them.

Scrooge   And is this my punishment? That I am left, feeble and alone?

Ghost of Christmas Future   No.

Sound from off. Children whispering, excited.

Ghost of Christmas Future   No, not quite.

Scrooge   Who's there?

Ghost of Christmas Future   I wish your ending could be that . . . peaceful.

Two children – the boy and girl who would have been **Scrooge** *and* **Belle**'s *children – enter. Now they are* **Ignorance** *and* **Want**. *They are dressed in rags.*

Scrooge   Hello there! Young man, young lady! You have no idea how glad I am to see you both.

The children circle around him, not coming close.

Ignorance   See anyone else?

Want   Not a soul. He's alone.

Scrooge   That's right, children, quite alone.

The children stop prowling, focus on **Scrooge** *now.*

Ghost of Christmas Future   Do you recognise them, Scrooge?

Scrooge   I take little note of urchins on the streets.

Ignorance   You look sick, mister.

Scrooge   No, I'm not sick – I'm just old.

Ignorance   Old?

Scrooge   Old and weak. I can't even get up from this chair.

Ignorance *and* **Want** *look at each other. They smile.*

Ghost of Christmas Future   You should take note of these two.

They're moving towards **Scrooge**, *studying him.*

Scrooge   And why's that?

Ghost of Christmas Future   Because these children are yours.

Scrooge   Mine? Nonsense.

They're sniffing him, examining him.

Want   Like your hat, mister.

Scrooge   Well, that's very nice of you to say. Now, I'm going to need your help. Could you go and fetch your mother, or father? I don't mind which.

Ignorance   Don't know my mum. Nor my dad.

Want   Like your hat *a lot*, mister.

Scrooge   Yes, you mentioned.

Want   I think I want it.

Scrooge   Well, if you work very hard and save up perhaps you could buy one –

Want   Think I'll have it now.

She snatches **Scrooge***'s hat.*

Scrooge   You can't do that!

Ignorance   Why not?

Scrooge   Because it's against the law.

Ignorance What's the law?

Scrooge The law of the land!

Ignorance What's the land?

Scrooge This place. This place where we are, now, all of us.

Ignorance What's 'us'?

Scrooge Us – you, me, them, everybody.

Want And I want your watch, mister. Think I'll have that.

Scrooge You give that back!

Ignorance Why give it back?

Want Know what else I want? I want your house. So I think I'll have that.

Ghost of Christmas Future These children are yours, Scrooge. You raised them.

Want I haven't got a house. I want one. I'll have yours.

Ghost of Christmas Future The girl is Want.

Ignorance Why can't she have your house? Why? Why?

Ghost of Christmas Future The boy is Ignorance.

Scrooge Aren't there places for you to go? Are children not cared for?

Want There's prison.

Ignorance And the workhouse. Workhouse is horrible. We'll stay here.

Ghost of Christmas Future You made them who they are.

Want You know what else I want? I want all your things. I want everything you own, I want everything you own!

Scrooge You can't just break into people's houses and take whatever you want!

Ignorance   Why not?

Scrooge   Because it's against the law –

Ignorance   What's law?

Scrooge   Oh no, we've tried that. Because it's wrong.

Ignorance   What's wrong?

Scrooge   This is!

Ignorance   What?

Scrooge   THIS!

Ghost of Christmas Future   You would not provide for them – and so they learned to provide for themselves. You taught them to prey on the weak. You taught them that the law protected the rich, and kept down the poor. You taught them how to make their way in the world – like every good father should.

Want   We've got a system. We find what we want – and we take it. And guess what?

Want *and* **Ignorance** (*sing*)
    The system works, the system works, the system works.

Want   You know what else I want? I want a daddy.

Ignorance   What's a daddy?

Want   This man. This man's our daddy.

Ignorance   What does a daddy do?

Want   He gives you everything you want. You can play with him. You can have all sorts of fun!

Ignorance   Can I play with him?

Want   Play all you like!

Ignorance *whoops and yells, pushing* **Scrooge***'s chair around the stage.*

Scrooge   Help! Help me! Somebody!

Want *is touring* **Scrooge**'s *room, picking up everything she wants, climbing on to his throne, tearing it down, picking through the wreckage. As she goes, she's chanting from* **Scrooge**'s *song, 'I'm the Man You Turn To'.*

Want
    I want your bread, I want your wine,
    I want your cows, I want your swine,
    I want your spade, I want your pick,
    I want your mortar and your brick – (*And so on.*)

Ignorance   Let's play horsey!

He tips **Scrooge** *out of the chair, on to the floor – and then leaps on his back.*

Ignorance   Giddy-up! Giddy-up, horsey!

Want *discovers a chest full of gold coins. She tips them out.*

Want   And I want *all* of this.

Scrooge *struggles to speak with* **Ignorance** *sitting on him.*

Scrooge   No, that's mine, please, that's all my savings!

Ignorance   Let's play – war!

Scrooge   War?

Ignorance   War!

Scrooge   I can't! I don't know how to play war!

Ignorance   Nor do I! I'm making it up as I go! But I bet it means –

He finds **Tiny Tim**'s *crutch among* **Scrooge**'s *things.*

Ignorance   – beating you with this till you're completely dead! Hooray!

He sets about **Scrooge** *with the crutch.*

Scrooge (*as he's being beaten*)   Spirit, show some mercy! Please! For pity's sake!

Ghost of Christmas Future   And what have you done to deserve pity, Scrooge?

Scrooge *struggles for an answer. But cannot find one.*

Scrooge   Nothing at all!

Ghost of Christmas Future   Then why should I save you?

Scrooge   Because of Christmas. Because it is a day of peace, and love, and goodwill to all men, whether they deserve it or not!

Ghost of Christmas Future   Then it is done!

The chaos onstage comes to an instant halt and everything goes black.

Scrooge   Hello?

Light on **Scrooge**, *still lying on the floor.*

Hello?

Light on the rest of the stage. He is alone in his home.

Have they truly gone? Now, let's see if I can . . .

He tries to get up. He can!

I have my strength back! I am my old self again!

He brushes himself down.

But no! Not my old self, not quite.

Outside a **Boy** *saunters past, singing a carol to himself.*

Scrooge   You! Boy!

Boy   Sorry, sir! Sorry, Mr Scrooge! I won't sing again, sir!

Scrooge   Tell me, lad, what day is this?

Boy   What day, sir?

Scrooge   Yes, my fine fellow.

Boy   It's Christmas Day!

Scrooge   Christmas Day?

Boy   Yes, sir, and the clocks just called ten in the morning.

Scrooge   I have the day again! I have my whole life again!

Boy   Are you quite all right, Mr Scrooge, sir?

Scrooge   I am as light as a feather, I am as happy as an angel, I am as merry as a schoolboy. Do you know the poulterer's in the next street but one, on the corner?

Boy   I should hope I did.

Scrooge   An intelligent boy! A remarkable boy! Do you know whether they've sold the prize turkey that was hanging up there – not the little prize turkey, the big one?

Boy   What, the one as big as me?

Scrooge   Yes, my buck – now go and buy it, bring it to me, and I'll give you a shilling. Be back in less than five minutes and I'll give you half a crown.

He begins to put on his hat and coat – but implausibly speedily, the **Boy** *returns, carrying a massive turkey.*

Scrooge   That was very quick!

Boy   I ran, sir.

Scrooge   You ran? Ingenious! Here's your half-crown.

He hands over a coin – and produces another.

Now, would you care to run another errand, and make your half a whole?

Boy   Yes please, sir.

Scrooge   I need you to go to the house of my nephew Fred. I'll give you his address –

Boy   Fred Scrooge? Everyone knows him, sir.

Scrooge   Do they?

Boy   The kindest man in all London, they say.

Scrooge   Is he really? Well, you go and tell Fred, his uncle will be joining him for Christmas supper.

He hands over the second coin.

Boy   Consider it done, sir!

And the **Boy** *shoots off.* **Scrooge** *picks up the turkey –*

Scrooge   Now you come with me, magnificent bird.

– and walks to the **Cratchits**'.

Scrooge   Hello! Hello?

Mrs Cratchit   Who's that?

Bob Cratchit   I fear I know the voice . . .

Scrooge   I'll play a trick on him! (*Calling, stern.*) Mr Bob Cratchit! It is your employer, Mr Scrooge. I demand you face me at once!

Bob Cratchit *goes to investigate.*

Bob Cratchit   Mr Scrooge, sir, it is Christmas, I am permitted a holiday . . .

He sees the turkey.

Mr Scrooge?

Scrooge   Merry Christmas, my dear man! And merry Christmas to all your family. I hoped I might join you for dinner.

Bob Cratchit   You're welcome to, sir.

Mrs Cratchit, *still inside, can't see* **Scrooge**.

Mrs Cratchit   We've got little enough as it is!

Scrooge   I hope it is not overly bold, but I took the liberty of bringing a bird with me.

The **Cratchits** *rush to see.*

Tiny Tim   That turkey's bigger than I am!

Bob Cratchit What do you say, Mrs Cratchit?

Mrs Cratchit I say . . . it may take some time to cook, Mr Scrooge, sir.

Scrooge If we have to wait while the bird is baked, we can divert ourselves . . . with a game.

All the Cratchits A game?

Scrooge Or a song?

All the Cratchits A song?

Scrooge I believe carols are popular at Christmas?

All the Cratchits CAROLS?

Scrooge Am I wrong, is that not the thing? I am a relative newcomer to Christmas-keeping.

Bob Cratchit No, carols are the done thing, you are entirely correct. It is simply – you are much changed, Mr Scrooge.

Mrs Cratchit It is perfectly obvious. Mr Scrooge has been visited by the Spirit of Christmas, it's plain to see.

Scrooge Indeed, good lady, I have been visited by all three of them. And very grateful I am for their lessons. And from this day forward I will live with the kindness and warmth and love of Christmas in my heart not just on Christmas Day, but on every day.

Tiny Tim But what are we going to sing?

They all begin to argue and squabble over which carol to sing. **Marley** *enters.*

Marley And so it was that Ebenezer Scrooge became as good a friend, as good a master, and as good a man, as the good old city knew, or any other good old city, town or borough, in the good old world. He became a second father to Tiny Tim, who did not die, but grew to become a strong and kind man, loved by all.

Scrooge and Belle became firm friends, and he saw to it that Belle's sister was cared for. It was always said of Scrooge that he knew how to keep Christmas well, if any man alive possessed the knowledge. And as Scrooge changed his ways, I cast off my chains, and was permitted entry into Heaven. And so, as Tiny Tim observed:

Tiny Tim   God bless us, every one!

Mrs Cratchit   Are we finally in accord?

Scrooge   I think so, good lady. Let's see if we can also be in harmony!

The **Cratchits** *groan at the awful joke.*

All the cast sing 'Good King Wenceslas', **Scrooge** *becoming the king,* **Bob Cratchit** *the page, and* **Tiny Tim** *the peasant. The rest are a chorus.*

Chorus
   Good King Wenceslas looked out
   On the Feast of Stephen,
   When the snow lay round about,
   Deep and crisp and even.
   Brightly shone the moon that night,
   Though the frost was cruel,
   When a poor man came in sight,
   Gathering winter fuel.

Scrooge
   Hither, page, and stand by me,
   If thou know'st it, telling –
   Yonder peasant, who is he?
   Where and what his dwelling?

Bob Cratchit
   Sire, he lives a good league hence,
   Underneath the mountain;
   Right against the forest fence,
   By Saint Agnes' fountain.

Scrooge

Bring me flesh, and bring me wine,
Bring me pine logs hither:
Thou and I will see him dine,
When we bear them thither.

Chorus

Page and monarch, forth they went,
Forth they went together;
Through the rude wind's wild lament
And the bitter weather.

Bob Cratchit

Sire, the night is darker now,
And the wind blows stronger;
Fails my heart, I know not how;
I can go no longer.

Scrooge

Mark my footsteps, good my page.
Tread thou in them boldly;
Thou shalt find the winter's rage
Freeze thy blood less coldly.

Chorus

In his master's steps he trod,
Where the snow lay dinted;
Heat was in the very sod
Which the saint had printed.
Therefore, Christian men, be sure,
Wealth or rank possessing,
You who now will bless the poor,
Shall yourselves find blessing.

All come together to repeat the last line.

All

You who now will bless the poor,
Shall yourselves find blessing.